William Wallace and Robert the Bruce: The Lives of Scotland's Most Famous Military Heroes

By Charles River Editors

A statute commemorating Wallace at the Scottish National Portrait Gallery in Edinburgh

About Charles River Editors

Introduction

Early 20th century depiction of Wallace in H E Marshall's *Scotland's Story*.

William Wallace (?-1305)

"A false usurper sinks in every foe

And liberty returns with every blow." – Blind Harry

From their very beginnings, England and Scotland fought each other. Emerging as unified nations from the early medieval period, their shared border and inter-related aristocracy created endless causes of conflict, from local raiders known as border reivers to full blown wars between their monarchies. Every century from the 11th to the 16th was colored by such violence, and there were periods when not a decade went by without some act of violence marring the peace.

Out of all of this, the most bitterly remembered conflict is Edward I's invasion during the late 13th century. After Edward's death, the English were eventually beaten back at the famous Battle of Bannockburn in 1314, and thus the early 14th century was a period featuring some of Scotland's greatest national heroes, including William Wallace and Robert the Bruce. It still resonates in the Scottish national memory, all the more so following its memorable but wildly inaccurate depiction in the 1995 film *Braveheart*, which had Scottish audiences cheering in cinemas.

William Wallace is one of the most famous freedom fighters in history, and over 700 years after his death he is still remembered as Scotland's beloved hero. But while the movie *Braveheart* helped make him a household name, and he is commemorated across Scotland as a natural leader and a loyal son of his homeland, he is also "the most mysterious of the leaders of the Scottish resistance to Edward I."[1] This is because, paradoxically, the very famous soldier is also one of the least well known. In fact, the mystery surrounding Wallace is figuring out precisely, or even vaguely, who he was. Where did this champion of Scottish independence come from? Who was his family? What did he do before emerging from obscurity with the brutal murder of William Heselrig, the English sheriff of Lanark, in May 1297? So little evidence on Wallace's life exists that answering even the most basic questions about him can be a challenge.

That said, as one scholar perceptively notes, "the facts are not the reason why he is remembered as a meaningful historical actor." [2] For the admirers Wallace has accumulated over the centuries, the idealized version of what he stood for - weak over strong, justice over injustice, the will of the people over the might of the powerful - is infinitely more important than the historical man himself. Similarly, his English detractors have also focused on image over substance through the years, depicting Wallace as a heartless brute, a cruel traitor, and a blood-hungry outlaw. Whether he's depicted as an icon of Scottish resistance or a symbol of disloyalty and treachery, William Wallace is as much an idea as he was an actual figure of the Scottish Wars of Independence.

Piecing together the story of William Wallace's life is an exercise in asking more questions than can be answered, and often in looking at just as much conjecture as proof. This book attempts to separate fact from fiction while looking at the life and fighting of the man who inspired *Braveheart*. Along with pictures and a bibliography, you will learn about William

---

[1] Michael Prestwich, "Review of *William Wallace* by Andrew Fisher," *The American Historical Review*, Vol. 93, No. 5 (Dec., 1988), p. 1312.

[2] G. Morton. *William Wallace: Man and Myth* (Stroud, 2001).

Wallace like you never have before.

Robert the Bruce (1274-1329)

A statue of Robert the Bruce at Bannockburn

Though it's often forgotten today, Robert the Bruce was a bit shiftier, if only out of necessity. Robert the Bruce has become a figure of Scottish national legend, renowned as the man who threw off the shackles of English oppression, but prior to 1306, this Anglo-Scottish nobleman did little to cover himself in glory or to earn a reputation as a hero of the national cause. A member of one of Scotland's leading noble families, Bruce inherited his grandfather's claim to the right to be King of the Scots. That older Bruce had been one of the two leading competitors in the Great

Cause, and the family still held ambitions toward the throne. They also held resentments dating back to that disputed inheritance against the Balliol clan and their supporters the Comyns.

Of course, this was all forgiven and forgotten after Bannockburn and Bruce's rise to the Scottish throne, which he held for over two decades. This book analyzes the life of Robert the Bruce and the events that led to his rise as the most famous Scottish king of the Middle Ages. Along with pictures of important people, places, and events, you will learn about Robert the Bruce and the Scottish Wars of Independence like never before.

William Wallace and Robert the Bruce: The Lives of Scotland's Most Famous Military Heroes

About Charles River Editors

Introduction

Chapter 1: Blind Harry and Wallace's Early Years

It is impossible to discuss William Wallace without making reference to Blind Harry, or Henry the Minstrel (c.1440-c.1492), the 15th century bard credited with writing the earliest surviving account of Wallace's life: the epic poem "The History of the Life and Heroic Actions of the Renowned Sir William Wallace, General and Governor of Scotland." Written somewhere around 1474-1479, roughly 170 years after the warrior's death, the epic contains more than 11,000 lines on Wallace's exploits and is peppered with a great deal of embellishment and fiction. But despite the fact it is heavily scrutinized over its accuracy (or lack thereof), Blind Harry's epic has framed the way the Scottish warrior is remembered and has shaped what many think of as the "historical" Wallace.

15th century financial accounts show that Blind Harry earned a living reciting poetry and song and had performed in the court of King James IV, as well as other noble venues. Thus, not surprisingly, the Wallace he depicts is a blend of folklore and literary conventions deliberately intended to portray the warrior as a "gracious god of Scotland," rather than some ordinary Scotsman from a middling-rank noble family.[3] It is also important to note that Harry performed mainly for anti-English audiences who were hungry for tales of rebellion and misdeeds against their southern neighbor. Moreover, many nobles found in Harry's work the opportunity to attack the reigning Scottish monarch, King James III, who was perceived as supporting pro-English policies far too much. Having Harry recite his heavily anti-English biography of Wallace was likely a way for many Scottish nobles of the 1470s to promote indirect criticism of James III.

---

[3] John Balaban, "Blind Harry and 'The Wallace'" *The Chaucer Review*, Vol. 8, No. 3 (Winter, 1974), p. 250.

Portrait of James III, King of Scots

Whatever their motives, Scottish nobles taking in Harry's epic would have heard of a robust and indefatigable Wallace, a Scottish hero who wanted nothing other than to destroy the hated English. He was a larger-than-life champion who made the ultimate sacrifice for his people: "Thus, we have a heroic figure in size and deed, who gave his life to his country – Right sooth it is, a martyr Wallace was." With lines like that, it's easy to understand how Harry's Wallace would appeal to the Scots and the anti-English sentiments that prevailed in the 1470s, but what might have surprised even Harry himself is the lasting appeal his work on Wallace would come to have on the Scots for centuries after his death. Since the 1470s, Blind Harry's biography has constituted the popular version of Wallace's life and was even the template for the 1995 film

Braveheart. It also helped that an adaptation of the poem was completed by William Hamilton and published in 1722, making Harry's work more accessible to a broader audience.[4] Indeed, it was this later version that fueled the imagination of many writers and poets, including the 18th century Scottish poet Robert Burns, whose 1793 patriotic song "Scots Wha Hae," or "Scots, who have," begins with the line "Scots, who have with Wallace bled."

Despite its enduring popularity, Harry's epic retelling of Wallace's deeds is barely recognizable when it comes to history, as it is undoubtedly more fiction than fact. Nevertheless, by virtue of its long-standing prevalence, the Wallace it depicts is the Wallace of the popular imagination. Thus, to arrive at a more authentic view of the "real" Scottish leader, historians must first dismantle the legend.

The process of distinguishing fact from fiction in Wallace's life begins with the Scot's origins and family. It was long thought, based on Blind Harry's account, that Wallace's father was a certain Malcolm who came from the area of Renfrew, west of Glasgow. The genealogies constructed around this claim declare Wallace to be the great-great-grandson of Richard Wallace, a vassal to Walter Fitzalan. In 1136, Fitzalan entered the service of David I, king of Scotland, as a steward of the household, and Richard Wallace is presumed to have been part of a flood of English-born men who followed Fitzalan (also English) north to serve the Scottish monarchy. Though the exact date of Richard's move to Scotland is unknown, most believe it took place during the reign of Walter I, which began in 1166.

It is believed that Wallace's father Malcolm had at least five children, including William, his two brothers John and Malcolm (at least one of whom was older than William), and possibly two sisters as well. As a younger son, Wallace could not inherit the family estate and thus would have had to seek a living beyond his kin. One of Blind Harry's best-known claims was that Wallace had planned for a life in the Church, a common vocational choice for younger sons. Tutored by a maternal uncle who was a priest, Wallace, Blind Harry boasted, was extremely well educated, knew both Latin and Greek, and possessed a particularly profound knowledge of the Bible. In this telling, William's progress toward the contemplative life would have proceeded uninterruptedly if only Edward I of England had not set out to bring Scotland under his domination. Enraged by the monarch's actions, Wallace abandoned his plans of joining the Church and began his famous fight against the English, a fight that made him one of Scotland's most celebrated figures.

---

[4] James E. Fraser, "'A Sawn from a Raven': William Wallace, Brucean Propaganda, and "Gesta Annalia" II," *The Scottish Historical Review*, Vol. 81, No. 211, (April, 2002), p. 1.

Portrait of Edward I of England

Blind Harry's version of Wallace's early years is unquestionably an absorbing narrative, especially the future leader's dramatic shift from tranquil preparation for life in the church to the tooth-and-nail existence of a warrior, and over the centuries, this extraordinary story has been the definitive account of the hero's early life. It was believed to be wholly credible largely because Harry himself had claimed to have based his account of Wallace on a Latin prose description of the warrior's life written by one of his contemporaries, John Blair. A Benedictine monk, Blair is understood to have been Wallace's personal chaplain, and he later wrote extensively about his famous patron. Though his work has long been lost, Blind Harry's presumed access to the writings of one of Wallace's contemporaries lent great legitimacy to his own work, since it was assumed the bard was drawing from an informed and authentic source.[5]

However, since so much of Wallace's life as told by Blind Harry has turned out to be more myth than fact, most scholars now dismiss every aspect of Harry's poem, which leaves almost nothing known for sure about Wallace's origins, family, and early years. As historian Andrew Fisher put it, William Wallace is "at best a shadowy figure and likely to remain so."[6] Besides a rough estimate of his birth year, which most believe to be around 1270, specific details, such as place of birth, exact date of birth, or the location and condition of the Wallace family, remain elusive.

Why have historians cast aside Blind Harry's account of Wallace's family? The discovery of new and, according to Fisher, "indisputable" evidence shows that Wallace was not the son of Sir Malcolm Wallace of Elderslie in Renfrew but of a certain Alan Wallace. On becoming Guardian of Scotland following the battle of Stirling Bridge in 1297, Wallace sent letters to the public officials of the German towns of Lübeck and Hamburg for the purpose of recommencing trade with the Hanseatic League, and one of these missives, known as the Lübeck letter, has survived.[7] It is one of the few surviving artifacts that can be connected to Wallace, and most importantly, Wallace used a seal on the letter containing the following inscription: "[Wilelm]vs Filius Alani Walais" (William, son of Alan Wallace). The inscription was a clear indication of the father's name.[8]

This revelation about Wallace's true parentage undermined centuries of studies about his family line (long linked to Malcolm and considered to be in the west of Scotland) and raises new possibilities about the Scottish hero's origins and early years. Of course, identifying precisely who Alan was has been historians' primary concern. The Ragman Roll of 1296, a collection of documents containing the names of the Scottish nobility and gentry who subscribed allegiance to King Edward I of England, provides a tantalizing clue. It lists an Alan Wallace as a landholder in Ayrshire, in southwest Scotland. If this Alan is indeed Wallace's father, then this raises numerous new questions about the Wallace clan and allows for a different picture of how Wallace spent his early years.

The most pressing question this piece of evidence raises has to do with the family's political loyalties. It has long been assumed that the Wallace clan was united in its anti-English sentiment and in its support of rebellion against Edward I, but if the Alan Wallace listed in the Ragman Roll was indeed Wallace's father, this evidence forces scholars to reconsider this notion. As hard as it may be to believe, the Ragman Roll begs the question of whether Wallace's own father supported Edward I. Otherwise, why would he pledge allegiance to Edward I by signing his name to this document?

---

[5] For a more extensive discussion of Blind Harry's work, see Graham McLennan, ed., *The Wild Flower: Blind Harry's Life of Wallace the Outlaw* (Caberra, 1993).

[6] Andrew Fisher, *William Wallace* (Edinburgh: John Donald Publishers, 1986).

[7] This letter is kept in the National Archives of Lübeck.

[8] Metal casts of the front and back of the seal were made in 1911. In 1999, they were discovered tucked away in a small box in Glasgow's Mitchell Library.

It's altogether possible that the appearance of Alan Wallace's name on the Ragman Roll should not be taken to mean that he was opposed to the Scottish rebellion against Edward I. Like many Scots at this time, Alan was probably acting as a realist, toeing the line in order to protect his property and to survive in the challenging and quickly changing political context. What's more, signing the Ragman Roll was not necessarily a voluntary act, as many people were forced to put their names on it regardless of their actual political stance. It's possible the Wallace clan was united in its opposition to the English, and at the same time, the Alan listen in the Ragman Roll may not be the father of the famed William Wallace anyway.

The clues left by the seal Wallace used on the Lübeck letters are not related exclusively to his father, because the images it contains also reveal something about what the young Scotsman might have done before his meteoric rise to become Guardian of Scotland in 1297. While the front of the seal displays a Scottish Lion rampant (the Royal Arms of Scotland), the reverse shows a particularly telling image of a strung bow with an arrow. This does not appear to be part of a coat of arms, as the bow and arrow are not displayed on a shield, the usual device to convey heraldic imagery. Rather, the seal merely shows a hand drawing an arrow on a bow. Though Wallace's seal is small and the imagery on it is faint, it nonetheless casts strong doubt on Blind Harry's claim that prior to the Scottish Wars of Independence, Wallace was set to become a clergyman. It seems quite incongruous that someone bent on joining the Church would have a bow and arrow - symbols of warfare - as his seal, but as for the Wallace that the world is familiar with - the victor at Stirling Bridge, the brazen rebel against the English - the bow and arrow make perfect sense. It was also in line with the physical descriptions of Wallace spread during the 15th century. While it's highly unlikely Wallace was 7 feet tall as suggested by Harry, an abbot named Walter Bower described him at least a bit more realistically as "a tall man with the body of a giant ... with lengthy flanks ...broad in the hips, with strong arms and legs ... with all his limbs very strong and firm". This would certainly be in line with a professional soldier, and had the young Wallace earned his living through the bow and quiver, as the seal strongly indicates, it follows that one day he would emerge a great warrior, the colossal figure who routed the mighty English army in 1297.

What did it mean to earn one's living through the bow and quiver? One possibility is that Wallace was an outlaw, a suggestion many of his detractors made over the years. Another, and more plausible, likelihood is that the young Wallace made his way as a mercenary soldier, a profession many a younger son pursued and one that would help explain where he acquired the great military genius he showed in 1297 and 1298. In the late 13th century, there would have been several occasions for Wallace to find work as a soldier; at the time, Edward I was engaged in campaigns in France and in his successful effort to conquer Wales and incorporate it into the Kingdom of England. Either place would have provided Wallace the opportunity to hone his military skill. If he indeed did earn a living in the military, this would add an ironic twist to his life story, because it would likely mean the man who eventually crushed the English in 1297 acquired his military prowess from the very army he vanquished.[9]

While the notion of Wallace as a soldier fits well into his life narrative, it is, as are nearly all ideas about his early years, mere conjecture. Despite the new research possibilities the seal on the Lübeck letter opens, Wallace's origins and youth remain obscure, and efforts to reconstruct his lineage and early life are still just educated guessing games, bringing together and conjecturing about a handful of extant documents. What little is truly known about him relates primarily to the eight years between the Battle of Stirling Bridge in 1297 and his death in 1305. In this short window of time, William Wallace made himself known to posterity.

Chapter 2: Robert the Bruce's Early Years

Robert VII was born on July 11, 1274, probably at Turnberry Castle in Ayrshire. His parents had met and married the previous year on his father's return from crusade, after Robert VI brought Marjorie news of her husband's death on that same military campaign. Though it was a politically advantageous marriage, bringing together a family of grand title and one of great power, it seems to have been motivated by love. Young Robert was the first of eleven children - five sons and six daughters - who would between them come to include a King of Scotland, High King of Ireland and Queen of Norway.

As noble families went, the Bruces were something of a power house. Robert Bruce was a descendant of both the Gaelic nobility native to Scotland and the Anglo-Norman nobility that had become increasingly powerful in Scotland since the Norman conquest of England in 1066. Like many nobles of the period, he was descended from royalty, in his case King David I of Scotland, to whom he was connected on his father's side. First becoming established in Scotland in the early 12th century, the Bruces had come to dominate the southwest of the country, becoming one of the most powerful magnate families.

In fact, the future King Robert was one in a long line of men named Robert Bruce - alternatively Robert de Brus or Robert de Bruce, in the shifting spellings and naming conventions of the period. His grandfather and head of the family was Robert Bruce V, Lord of Annandale, the family's traditional base of power. His father, Robert Bruce VI, had married the widowed Marjorie, Countess of Carrick, and so become Earl of Carrick. This made him technically superior in rank to Robert V, but the Lord of Annandale remained leader of the Bruces.

There is little record of Robert VII's early years, and much of what we know comes not from direct accounts but from deductions based on his later life. It seems that he spent time with a foster family, a traditional practice among the Gaelic aristocracy, in which noble children would live for a while with another family, creating strong and lasting bonds of loyalty based on something other than blood. In keeping with a family that followed this tradition, he spoke

---

[9] For a discussion of the possibility that Wallace was a mercenary soldier in his youth, see Andrew Fisher, *William Wallace*, pp. 40-41.

Gaelic, the native language of the Highlands and western Scottish, as well as French - the language of the Norman-descended aristocracy - and Lowland Scots, which had evolved from a dialect of northern English. On top of these languages he was taught Latin, the language of scholarship, the church and much international diplomacy. He learnt to read and write, common but by no means universal skills among the aristocracy of the period, and later in life had books with him even while on the run. Perhaps the most important things he learnt were how to ride and how to fight, vital skills for a member of Europe's military aristocracy. That he was an able learner is demonstrated by his later battlefield prowess.

In 1286, at the age of 12, the young Robert acted in an adult capacity for the first time, when he was among the nobles witnessing a deed. It was the same year as the death of King Alexander III, an event that would propel Scotland into turmoil.

Chapter 3: England and Scotland

The English and Scottish monarchies had a complex relationship from the start. Both emerged from alliances and conquests of smaller kingdoms during the Dark Ages. By 1100, England had a stable established central monarchy which could assert authority over all of what now consists of the whole of England. The Kings of the Scots, on the other hand, were still struggling to dominate their supposed subjects in the north and west. Wales, the other portion of the island of Britain, had some sense of shared identity but a multiplicity of kings and princes who would periodically gain dominance over each other. In retrospect, it is possible to see that these nations had already established the outlines that would endure down the centuries, but at the time this could not be taken for granted.

One of the biggest issues was the feudal relationship between England and Scotland's monarchs, because it was not clear whether the King of Scots ruled as an independent king or as a sub-king of England, and neither side had sought to clarify this issue legally. For the Scots, to assert their complete independence would be to tempt English invasion, and for the English, it could stir up trouble to the north. Though their borders were frequent causes of dispute, and war erupted from time to time, relations in the mid-13th century were relatively stable.

In some minds, the relationship between the English and Scottish monarchies had been resolved in 1189 with the Quitclaim of Canterbury. Under this agreement, Richard I, more interested in funding his crusades than ruling in Britain, sold any English crown interests in Scotland for 10,000 marks. In reality, however, these matters could not be so smoothly settled because the ownership of lands by noble and royal families often changed down the generations, which meant many nobles held lands on both sides of the border. In the ever-shifting feudal landscape, there was no guarantee that such an agreement would not be surpassed by some other pact or marriage.

During the relatively weak reign of Henry III of England, Alexander II of Scotland gave up a

Scottish claim to disputed Northumberland in return for holding Penrith in Cumberland as a lordship under the English monarch. Alexander III, who inherited the Scottish throne in 1249, gave homage to Henry III for Penrith, but this exchange of a disputed claim for real lands, far from resolving the relationship between the two kingdoms, added to its complexity. The King of Scotland was now clearly a vassal of the King of England, at least in his role of Lord of Penrith.

A contemporary depiction of Henry III of England

A contemporary illustration depicting the coronation of Alexander III of Scotland

A portrait believed to depict Edward I of England

When Edward I became King of England in 1272, he sought to use this to his advantage by asserting that Alexander III should swear fealty to him due to his holdings as Lord of Penrith. Clear authority over his barons was very important to Edward, who had seen the English nobility rise up against his father in the 1260s and believed that an assertive approach was needed to keep the nobles in line. However, his attempt to assert dominance did not lead to recognition that he was overlord of Scotland and the superior of the two kings, so relations remained muddy (albeit amicable).

Chapter 4: A Scottish Succession Crisis

Ultimately, it was a succession crisis following the end of Alexander III's reign that gave Edward the opportunity he sought to gain control over the Scots, and he would push so far in asserting English dominance that the Scots were forced to resist or accept subservience to their southern neighbors.

Alexander III ruled Scotland from 1249 until his death in 1286, and like his father, Alexander II (1214-1249), he had maintained fairly good relations with England and focused most of his efforts on the more tenuous affairs with Norway. Following the Battle of Largs in 1263 and the death of the King of Norway shortly thereafter, Alexander claimed the Isle of Man and the Western Isles (the Outer Hebrides) for Scotland.

Alexander had three children by his first wife Margaret, who was none other than the daughter of Henry III of England and sister of Edward I, and one of these children (also named Margaret) married King Eric II of Norway. However, all of Alexander's children died in the early 1280s, leaving him without an heir and posing a serious problem for the Scots.

When the elder Margaret had died in 1275, Alexander hurried to find a new wife, but in the meantime, he had Princess Margaret, the Maid of Norway, named as his heir presumptive and thus his successor if another child was not born. Margaret, Alexander's granddaughter via his daughter Margaret and Eric II, was an infant living in Norway, and while her age, gender and location far from Scotland all made her an awkward choice, she was considered a better option than having a disputed succession that the English might capitalize on.

Still looking to provide a new heir, Alexander married Yolande de Dreux, Countess of Montfort, in November 1285, but the following March, while riding to visit Yolande, he fell from his horse and died of a broken neck. Alexander had acted impetuously in riding out alone into a dark and stormy night, and that action would now plunge his nation into turmoil.

Yolande was pregnant at the time of Alexander's death, but she miscarried soon after, so the three-year-old Margaret of Norway was left as Queen. With Margaret in no position to take the throne, she stayed in Norway while the Guardians of Scotland, a group of prominent magnates, ruled the country in her name.

Naturally, the power vacuum left by the absence of a monarch soon led to trouble. John Balliol, a prominent lord, tried to take the throne with the support of John Comyn, the head of one of the country's most powerful noble families, but the Bruce family, supported by others (including the Stewards), opposed the Balliols in Margaret's name and brought the rebellion to an end.

By 1289, the Guardians were maintaining an awkward peace between competing claims to the throne from the Balliols, Margaret of Norway, and the Bruces, and with so many others seeking to rule Scotland, none of them sought to bring Margaret to her new country, so she remained in Norway.

Nonetheless, Eric II of Norway wanted to see his daughter on the throne, and rather than attempt to do this with Scottish support, he went to Edward I for help. In 1289, the two kings entered negotiations for Margaret to marry Edward I's eldest son, the future Edward II, which would have made the future King of England also the King of Scotland and brought the two kingdoms together under a single dynasty with strong connections to Norway. The Scots were excluded from these negotiations until the Guardians met with Edward at Salisbury in October, but with no control over Margaret, they could do little to affect the discussions between Edward and Eric, so the future of their nation appeared out of their hands.

Still, the outcome of the talks at Salisbury was more favorable for them. It was eventually decided that Margaret would be sent to Scotland by the start of November the following year, and that no decision would be made about her marriage until she arrived. Thus, the Scots would have their infant Queen, and with her some control over their destiny.

However, poor Margaret never reached Scotland, as she became ill during the sea crossing from Norway and died in the Orkney Islands on September 26, 1290. The question of who would rule Scotland was now wide open, and more than any other person involved, King Edward I would drive the war that was about to break out between England and Scotland. His actions would earn him the title Hammer of the Scots, and his name would go down in infamy north of the border.

Despite everything that had come between them, relations between England and Scotland were friendly at the time of the Maid of Norway's death. The two royal families had strong connections through marriage, and there had even been an attempt to unite them by marrying the young Queen Margaret to Prince Edward. It was therefore a natural step for the Scots to involve Edward, as their southern neighbor and a man noted for his legal and decision making abilities, to settle their disputed succession.

Following Margaret's death, many contenders had come forward to lay claim to the throne of Scotland, a dispute known to history as the Great Cause, and with so many vested interests, it was impossible for the Scottish lords to decide the matter among themselves. Even in 1292, the throne still remained unoccupied, and there was no resolution in sight. It was the sort of difficult situation that produced civil wars, which was exactly what the Scottish leaders wanted to avoid.

Thus, the nobility of Scotland invited Edward to settle the Great Cause. He gathered them at Norham in Northumberland, in English territory but close to the Scottish border, and had the nobles present their cases so that he could choose the rightful king from among them. Of course, Edward's main aim in accepting this task was to have his position as overlord of Scotland acknowledged by the Scottish lords, making it a reality and not just a claim on his part. It was a similar issue to the one that had led to his invasion of Wales; he didn't necessarily want to rule directly, but he wanted whoever did the ruling to recognize his lordship over them.

However, while Edward saw himself as a monarch arbitrating between his subjects, the Scots saw him as a neighbor helping out during their time of crisis. The Scots avoided acknowledging Edward's sovereignty by saying that only a king could establish such a relationship, and so they could not recognize Edward's ongoing authority until the Great Cause was settled. That said, in the meantime, they acknowledged Edward as sovereign lord for the period during which their throne lay vacant.

Though there were 14 claimants to the throne of Scotland, there were only two likely candidates with the lineage, wealth and political authority to lead the nation. Both were descendants of King David I and men of the cross-border Anglo-Scottish nobility, with lands and interests in both countries. One was John Balliol, a substantial baron in England whose wife was of Scottish royal blood. The other was Robert Bruce, the Lord of Annandale. After a long hearing, Edward decided in favor of Balliol, who was crowned King John I of Scotland on St Andrews Day, the holy day of Scotland's national saint.

A medieval depiction of John Balliol

Some historians argue that Edward chose Balliol figuring he would be a weak king, and tellingly, as part of his decision to place John I on the throne, Edward demanded that the new king pay homage to him, let Scots take disputed court cases to the English King for arbitration, and supply troops for Edward's armies in times of war. Balliol was willing to accept the throne on Edward's terms rather than see it go to one of the other contenders, so he agreed. By defining substantial details of his overlordship, Edward gave himself a way to assert authority over the client king, but that authority would soon prove cause for war.

Regardless, upon learning that he had failed in his claim, the ageing Robert Bruce V finally gave up on his attempts to become King of Scotland, and on November 7, he passed the claim to his son, Robert VI. However, this Robert lacked his father's grand ambition, so on November 9, he passed his own position as Earl of Carrick to his son, Robert VII. It was a title he had only ever held due to his marriage to Marjorie, and with her passing earlier that year, it was only appropriate that the earldom should go to their son.

Robert Bruce V's last political act was to reach out from retirement and ensure the election of a Bruce supporter, Thomas Dalton of Kirkudbright, as Bishop of Galloway in 1294, despite opposition from King John. But for the most part he was out of politics, as was his son, while Robert VII was becoming increasingly prominent. The young Bruce was confirmed as Earl of Carrick in a Scottish Parliament of August 1293, and afterwards went to visit his family's lands in England. King Edward allowed Robert loans from the Royal Exchequer, as he sought to win the friendship of the young Earl. This may have been part of a policy of undermining John Balliol by encouraging his opponents, creating cause for future English intervention in Scotland.

As effective head of the family, Robert was now responsible for the well being of his brothers and sisters. He provided Isabella with a fine selection of wedding gifts, including gowns, bed-linen and silverware. He also began a family of his own, marrying Isabella, daughter of the Earl of Mar, in 1295. Sadly Isabella died giving birth to their first and only child, a daughter named Marjorie, in 1296.

On Robert V's death, Robert VI returned from Norway. He was appointed governor of Carlisle by King Edward, one more act of favor toward King John's political opponents as trouble grew between the two nations.

Chapter 5: The Hammer of the Scots

Having placed conditions on John that made him Edward's feudal vassal, the English king set about making use of their newly defined relationship. He wanted to bring Scotland firmly under control, and his relationship with King John was the way to do that. In 1293, the Earl of Fife and head of the Macduff family took a legal appeal to Edward after he was impeached by the Scottish Parliament, and Edward summoned King John to Westminster to attend the appeal, a politically aggressive act. Not only was Edward interfering in Scottish law and politics by hearing the appeal, he was also forcing the Scottish king to come to him as a feudal inferior rather than agreeing to a meeting place as befitted two anointed kings. John went, and though he refused to take part in discussing the Macduff case, the very fact that he obeyed Edward's summons disturbed many in Scotland.

Two years later, Edward called upon John to fulfill the military part of his feudal duties.

Edward was gathering an army to take to Gascony, where he was fighting Philip IV of France, and he ordered King John to come to London with 20 of his lords to serve in that army. These demands completely undermined John's authority in Scotland, reinforcing the image of him as subservient to Edward rather than ruling independently in his own right. To obey was to concede this point, and John's failure to stand up to Edward raised opposition from Scottish nobles opposed to English overlordship. Unhappy with his increasingly compromised rule, in July 1295 they forced John to accept a council of 12 leading men who would help govern the kingdom. In practice, this was a new council of Guardians that was taking over the direction of Scotland from Balliol and making him a puppet ruler.

Since Edward had asserted his rights over Scotland, the Scots needed to assert their independence more firmly or risk seeing it whittled away, so they allied with the French, beginning the series of treaties known as the Auld Alliance, in which the French and Scots regularly promised to back each other against the English. This move directly challenged all claims Edward had over Scotland, but the French king did not engage in this alliance for altruistic purposes. He shared Scotland's desire to curtail English expansion, but he also shared England's desire to exercise influence over Scotland. Furthermore, upon signing the Auld Alliance, it was decided that King Philip's niece would marry the heir to the Scottish throne, King John Balliol's son Edward. In the end, the marriage never took place, but the marriage agreement itself reveals the pragmatic political ploys typical of medieval Europe.

When Edward learned of the secret Franco-Scottish alliance, he began preparing his forces to attack Scotland while also fortifying his northern defenses and solidifying relations with various anti-Balliol Scots, most notably Robert Bruce. Following the outcome of the Great Cause, the Bruce clan had refused to support John Balliol's kingship, but it also remained close with Edward. In retaliation for Bruce's resistance, King John seized the Bruce family estates in Carrick in southwest Scotland and gave them to John Comyn. Thus, it likely came as no surprise to King John that his directive to all able-bodied Scotsmen to bear arms and assemble at Caddonlee near the English border in March 1296 and prepare for war with England went ignored by Robert Bruce. War had come between England and Scotland, and the Bruces were on the English side.

Edward had shown how little tolerance he had for dissent, and he had made clear that he considered Scotland a vassal kingdom with an underling king who owed him obedience. Just as he had acted when faced with resistance in Wales, Edward mustered his armed forces and marched. Moreover, Scotland was not united in the face of English aggression. Many nobles, including the Bruces, sided with Edward. Some of their reasons were political, as in the Bruce family's claim to the Scottish throne, but for others it was a matter of vested economic interests, as they held land on both sides of the border and might have their English territory confiscated if they opposed Edward. Some were merely bowing to the inevitable rather than oppose the stronger English. Between this collaboration and Scotland's military weakness relative to

England, Edward would never face much of a challenge.

The first move Edward made was against Berwick, where he had ordered King John to meet him. John, unsurprisingly, refused to do as he had been told to by a man whose authority he no longer recognized. When he didn't show up, Edward stormed Berwick, and many of its inhabitants were killed in a brutal massacre. Edward remained in Berwick for a month in the hopes of achieving a swift conquest of Scotland if not a full capitulation. However, on April 5, Edward received a communication from King John renouncing his fealty to the English monarch. The Scots were not yielding.

Edward subsequently focused on the next objective in his campaign: the castle at Dunbar, only a few miles up the coast from Berwick. The castle belonged to the Earl of March, who had sided with Edward, but his wife had remained a fierce patriot and allowed her fellow Scots to occupy the stronghold. Edward sent John Balliol's own father-in-law, John de Warenne, 6th Earl of Surrey, along with a bevy of knights (totaling about a third of the English army), northward to assess the castle. The Scots immediately sent word to King John, who was camped with the main army inland near Haddington, requesting reinforcements. John sent most of the army to rescue Dunbar, but rather than saving the castle, they suffered a speedy and humiliating defeat. Though the Scots had an advantageous position on high ground, they misjudged the English army's actions. Mistakenly thinking they were retreating, the Scots charged downhill in a confused fashion, leaving the safety of the hill behind them. They encountered the English in formation and were routed immediately on April 27, 1296. In addition to the casualties, the disaster resulted in at least 100 lords, knights and soldiers taken prisoner, including John Comyn, who was taken with the others to England.

With the Scottish army now virtually annihilated, Edward soon took the castles at Roxburgh, Edinburgh, Stirling, and Perth. Some, perhaps most famously Roxburgh, were surrendered with only the smallest attempt at a defense, while Edinburgh castle withstood for a week against Edward's siege machines. The English found Stirling castle completely abandoned, save for a caretaker who stayed back to leave the keys with the invading army. As these strongholds fell with ease into Edward's hand, the war was effectively over only a few months after it had begun. All that remained was for King John to surrender.

Following this quick succession of surrenders, John and some remaining lords fled to northeast Scotland, but it was soon clear to all that the Scottish monarch had no choice but to admit defeat and yield to Edward. On July 2, John officially begged forgiveness of Edward in a pleading letter. Edward accepted the surrender, but only after subjecting John to a humiliating ceremony on July 10, during which the deposed Scottish monarch had to renounce the treaty with France, apologize personally to Edward, and have the arms of Scotland formally stripped from his surcoat, earning him the nickname "Toom Tabard" ("empty coat"). John and his son Edward were transported to England, and John was imprisoned in the Tower of London until July 1299, when he was allowed to leave for France to be placed under the custody of Pope Boniface VIII.

After that, the victorious Edward was bent on destroying any remaining Scottish identity or hints of Scottish independence. He had records related to the Scottish throne sent to London, and, as a spoil of war, he captured the sacred Stone of Scone from Scone Abbey in Perth. The stone had been used for centuries as the seat of coronation for Scottish monarchs, but after Edward had it transported to Westminster Abbey in London, it was fitted into a wooden chair and used for the coronation ceremonies of the English monarchs, a potent symbol of England's claim over Scotland. Along with it, Edward also carted off the Scottish Crown Jewels and one of Scotland's holiest relics, the Black Rood of St. Margaret, which was believed to be a piece of the True Cross.

Edward's objective was nothing less than the destruction of Scotland and the total absorption of its people into his kingdom. To the latter end, he demanded oaths of fealty from Scots in acknowledgment of his overlordship. In late August 1296, nearly 1600 Scottish nobles and magnates made a personal oath to Edward by signing the Ragman's Roll, while any prominent Scot who failed to take this pledge was declared an outlaw and pursued by authorities.

Chapter 6: The Scottish Wars of Independence

As in Wales, resistance to Edward I had led to conquest and direct English rule, but unlike the Welsh, the Scots had not faced heavy losses in their defeat. Even the Battle of Dunbar was not a large engagement, and though it was demoralizing, it did little long-term damage to Scotland's military resources. The country might look beaten, but many Scots didn't yet feel that way.

Moreover, once he conquered the Scots, Edward I returned south; the Scottish campaign had drawn time and resources away from his war with the French, and he was determined to waste no more time, However, without the English King keeping them beneath his boot heel, and with much of his armed might drawn away to another war, the Scots found the will to resist.

Locked away in England, John Balliol was in no place to lead a fight back against the English, but he remained a figurehead to rally behind, and the Scots nobility began appointing sheriffs and other officials in his name, establishing their own resistance government. While a new government and administration was being pulled together, armed forces were being recruited to throw off the English yoke. This took place on three different fronts under different leaders. It had the most politically prominent and therefore legitimate leadership in the south-west, where a group of important lords and churchmen started gathering troops. Among them was Robert the Bruce, a grandson of the contender for the throne who would also eventually make his reputation fighting the English. In the northeast, Andrew Murray, having escaped English imprisonment after Dunbar, led the fight. Between them, in the center of the country, forces were gathered by the man who become the most famous leader of this period: William Wallace.

Contrary to popular myth, Wallace was not a peasant or common man. An obscure member of a minor noble family, his social status was always likely to lead him to the life of a man-at-arms, the battlefield role of the upper classes. He had deeper Scottish connections than the more prominent nobles, having been raised speaking Scots in a Scottish community rather than in the French-speaking cross-border Anglo-Scottish upper nobility. Still, Wallace would likely have remained an obscure figure, long forgotten by history, if not for his loyal adherence to the Balliol cause. Even in Scotland's darkest hour, he stood by the absent king, rallying armed forces in support of his claim to the throne. Whatever mixture of charisma and local influence allowed him to do it, Wallace gathered troops around him and led a series of successful hit-and-run raids against the occupiers. His adherence was vital to keeping the Balliol cause alive, but that cause was also vital to him and provided a status he would otherwise have lacked.

As the flames of revolt spread across Scotland, Wallace entered the fray, and though hard facts about his initial war efforts are difficult to source, what is clear is that he emerged from obscurity in May 1297 by murdering the English sheriff of Lanark, William De Hesilrig. Heselrig was part of the English administration Edward had imposed on Scotland following his conquest the previous year, and at the head of this administration was John de Warenne, 6th Earl of Surrey, who had been Edward's chief lieutenant during the Battle of Dunbar. Assisting Warenne was Hugh of Cressingham, who served as treasurer.

Wallace's slaying of Heselrig in May marked an important turning point in the unrest, as what had previously been disjointed resistance turned into full-blown rebellion. As sheriff, Heselrig was a symbol of the repressive English authority, and at the time of his murder, he was in Lanark to hold an assize, a court session for the trial of civil or criminal cases. It would seem that Wallace chose his target and the occasion carefully, as the murder of an English official while he was exercising the king's legal authority over the Scots would have sent a powerful message to both the occupiers and the occupied.

Precisely what Wallace was doing in Lanark (in central Scotland) in May 1297 is unknown, but popular tradition claims he was there to seek personal revenge against Heselrig. The legend, stemming from Blind Harry's account of Wallace, holds that Heselrig had murdered Wallace's beloved Marion Braidfute, the heiress of Lamington, a village not far from Lanark. It is not clear whether Braidfute was Wallace's wife or mistress, but most historians treat the story of Wallace's hot-blooded, vengeful murder of Heselrig as myth and Marion Braidfute as part of this legend, since no evidence supports the personal vengeance claim. It is far more likely that Wallace's brutal murder of Heselrig was intended to send a chilling message to the English that no one, not even officials, would be spared in the mounting rebellion. The English declared Wallace an outlaw, but many Scots were inspired by his actions and joined his campaign. Immediately after Lanark, Wallace's forces grew, spurred on perhaps by the rumor that Edward was looking to suppress midland Scotland in order to force the men of that region into his army to fight against France.

In August 1297, Edward I headed off to fight in Flanders, leaving Surrey and his associates to deal with the supposedly beaten Scots. He could not afford to abandon his adherents north of the border to the rebels or allow his recent conquest to be undone, but he also could not abandon his existing plans against the French to deal with the growing revolt, as this would make the rebels look more credible. Thus, he left the war to his lieutenants this time, confident that they could crush the Scots without him.

In June 1297, the English, led by Henry Percy and Robert Clifford, crossed into Annandale from Cumberland and burnt Lochmaden on their way to Irvine. A Scottish army under the leadership of Douglas, Robert Wishart (the bishop of Glasgow), James Stewart (one of the former Guardians of Scotland), and a recent convert to the patriotic cause, Robert the Bruce, gathered to face the English threat. Not long after the English cavalry advanced against them, the Scots sought to negotiate terms of surrender, but the negotiations were unusually lengthy, a fact that has led some historians to argue that the negotiated surrender was merely a ruse to give Wallace more time to assemble an army. Cressingham, Edward's treasurer, distrusted the Scots and raised an army to fight Wallace, but he was stopped by Percy and Clifford, who believed they had successfully pacified Scotland south of Lanark.

As it turned out, the English military leaders had underestimated their opponents. Following the capitulation at Irvine in July 1297, the Scots failed to surrender the hostages they had promised the English, and Stewart and Bruce rejoined the Scottish forces only a short time later. Wallace had since left the Forest of Selkirk to head north, where, according to Blind Harry, he burnt 100 English ships. Historian Andrew Fisher believes that was more likely the work of Andrew Murray, but either way, Wallace went on to push out the English from Fife and Perthshire. By August, he was laying siege to Dundee, and according to the chronicler Walter of Guisborough, Wallace had attained a large and diverse following: "the common folk of the land followed him as their leader and ruler; the retainers of the great lords adhered to him; and even though the lords themselves were present with the English king in body, at heart they were on the opposite side."By uniting their forces in a single army, Murray and Wallace signaled to the world that they believed they could beat the odds. That in the right circumstances, and with the right leadership, they could defeat the English in a pitched battle, striking a decisive blow for Scottish freedom.

The authority King Edward had reclaimed over Scotland the previous year was all but gone by the late summer of 1297. At the time, his treasurer, Cressingham, sent to his monarch the following assessment of the situation: "By far the greater part of your counties of the realm of Scotland are still unprovided with keepers...some have given up their bailiwicks, and others neither will nor dare return; and in some counties the Scots have established and placed bailiffs and ministers, so that no county is in proper order, excepting Berwick and Roxburgh, and this only lately." Finally acknowledging that the Scottish rebellion was strong and growing, the English at last aimed to take firm action. Warenne, Edward's chief lieutenant who had succeeded at Dunbar in 1296, left Berwick and headed for Stirling with a sizeable army. Accompanied by Cressingham, they arrived near Stirling in early September.

Meanwhile, Wallace left the siege of the castle at Dundee to the town's inhabitants and also headed to Stirling, having joined forces with Andrew Murray, whose successful rebellion in the north of Scotland had severely weakened the English there. Together, the two headed what the English called "a very large body of rogues," and in early September they took up position on the southward-looking slope of the Abbey Craig, about a mile north of a narrow wooden bridge stretching across the River Forth. This bridge, situated near Stirling Castle, was highly strategic, because the river was too deep and wide to cross below Stirling, and to the west lay Flanders Moss, marshland that was impossible to cross with an army. Furthermore, Stirling Bridge tied the north and south of Scotland together, so whoever controlled this site would hold a strategic advantage over the opponent.

Stirling Bridge today, with a monument to Wallace in the background

A picture of the northern side across the Stirling Bridge where Wallace's army was located. Photo by Kim Traynor.

Wallace and Murray, even with their entire Scottish army in the field, were about to face a test of strength. The English army, with its heavy cavalry, outnumbered the Scots by a comfortable margin, a fact that might have caused Warenne to expect another easy victory like at Dunbar. He and Cressingham also had the advantage of experience on their side, since neither Wallace nor Murray could claim extensive military practice and neither had ever before commanded a large force. However, despite these clear advantages, Warenne did not seem bent on engaging in battle. In the days before the battle, he sent representatives to negotiate the surrender of the Scots, and when that failed, he sent two Dominican friars as envoys to speak with Wallace and

Murray in order to procure from them terms for surrender. Much to Warenne's surprise, he received in response not a capitulation, but Wallace's well-known rebuff: "Go back and tell your people that we have not come here for peace: we are ready, rather, to fight to avenge ourselves and to free our country. Let them come up to us as soon as they like, and they will fund us prepared to prove the same in their beards."

Hearing Wallace's slight, Warenne ordered an attack. Early on the morning of September 11, 1297, the English army, led by Cressingham, began to cross Stirling Bridge at a painstakingly slow pace, as the bridge was wide enough for only two horsemen to stand abreast. However, even after some 5,000 made it across, Warenne, who had overslept that morning and arrived late to the site, promptly recalled all of them. Warenne convened a Council of War, but he ignored the wise advice of a former Scottish knight, Richard Lundie, who had suggested crossing the river with his cavalry at a nearby ford where 60 horsemen could traverse together, in order to outflank the Scots. Cressingham preferred the bridge crossing, and Warenne deferred to his opinion.

As a result, within a few hours, the army again began a slow crossing of the bridge. Wallace and Murray observed the enemy's maneuvers from the Abbey Crag and waited until a certain number of the enemy had reached their side of the river. Once satisfied, they ordered their infantry down the slope along the narrow causeway to the bridge. The English cavalry, whose horses were unable to gain solid ground on the marshy terrain, floundered as the Scots seized the northern end of the bridge, thereby cutting off the advancing force from the rest of the army and from the hope of reinforcements. While the rest of the English army watched, the Scots annihilated or let drown some 5,000 infantry and 100 knights, including Cressingham, whose body was flayed and made into trophies. Tradition holds that Cressingham's skin was used to make Wallace's sword belt; the Lanercost Chronicle reported that Wallace had "a broad strip...taken from the head to the heel, to make therewith a baldrick for his sword."

While Cressingham and the men on the other side of the bridge suffered their grisly fates, Warenne never crossed the bridge. As he witnessed the slaughter of his men from afar, he now had to worry about preventing the Scots from crossing the river in pursuit of what remained of the English army, so Warenne ordered the bridge's destruction and then promptly fled back to Berwick.

Naturally, the battle is best remembered for the way in which Blind Harry described it, even as his fantastical account is filled with inaccuracies:

> "On Saturday they [Murray and Wallace] rode on to the bridge, which was of good plain board, well made and jointed, having placed watches to see that none passed from the army. Taking a wright, the most able workman there, he [Wallace] ordered him to saw the plank in two at the mid streit [middle stretch], so that no-one might walk over it. He then nailed it up quickly with hinges, and dirtied it with clay,

to cause it to appear that nothing had been done. The other end he so arranged that it should lie on three wooden rollers, which were so placed, that when one was out the rest would fall down. The wright, himself, he ordered to sit there underneath, in a cradle, bound on a beam, to loose the pin when Wallace let him know by blowing a horn when the time was come. No one in all the army should be allowed to blow but he himself.

The day of the great battle approached; for power, the English would not fail; they were ever six to one against Wallace. Fifty thousand made for the place of battle, the remainder abiding at the Castle; both field and Castle they thought to conquer at their will. The worthy Scots upon the other side of the river, took the plain field on foot.

Hugh Cressingham leads on the vanguard with twenty thousand likely men to see. Thirty thousand the Earl of Warren had, but he did then as wisdom did direct, all the first army being sent over before him. Some Scottish men, who well knew this manner of attack, bade Wallace sound, saying there were now enough. He hastened not, however, but steadily observed the advance until he saw Warren's force thickly crowd the bridge. Then from Jop he took the horn and blew loudly, and warned John the Wright, who thereupon struck out the roller with skill; when the pin was out, the rest of it fell down. Now arose an hideous outcry among the people, both horses and men, falling into the water. (...)

On foot, and bearing a great sharp spear, Wallace went amongst the thickest of the press. he aimed a stroke at Cressingham in his corslet, which was brightly polished. The sharp head of the spear pierced right through the plates and through his body, stabbing him beyond rescue; thus was that chieftain struck down to death. With the stroke Wallace bore down both man and horse.

The English army although ready for battle, lost heart when their chieftain was slain, and many openly began to flee. Yet worthy men abode in the place until ten thousand were slain. Then the remainder fled, not able to abide longer, seeking succour in many directions, some east, some west, and some fled to the north. Seven thousand full at once floated in the Forth, plunged into the deep and drowned without mercy; none were left alive of all that fell army."

Regardless of the subsequent embellishments, Wallace and Murray's achievement at Stirling Bridge was nothing less than remarkable. Despite their inferior numbers, and an army composed of a ragtag host of peasants, farmers and burgesses, the two leaders exploited the terrain and outwitted and outmaneuvered the far more experienced Warenne and his heavy cavalry. The effects of this resounding victory were felt immediately too. Dundee and Stirling castles surrendered, while the towns Edinburgh and Berwick also fell to the Scots (though their castles remained in English hands). When the towns of Haddington and Roxburgh were burnt, English hold over Scotland had been all but eliminated.

While the victory at Stirling Bridge decisively swung the war's momentum behind the Scots, it came at a cost. Andrew Murray was grievously injured during the battle and died in early November. Despite his injuries, over the two months between Stirling Bridge and his death, Murray and Wallace worked together as leaders not only of the Scottish army but of the country as a whole. In October, the two sent missives to the mayors and communes of Hamburg and Lübeck in an attempt to restore trading relations with Germany, and in early November, Wallace followed up this attempt at diplomacy by securing the election of William Lamberton, who turned out to be staunchly anti-English, as the bishop of St. Andrews. Around that time, Murray passed away from the wounds he had sustained at Stirling Bridge, leaving the burden of defending Scotland solely on Wallace's shoulders. For the next year, Wallace would hold the highest rank of power and authority in Scotland.

A stained glass depiction of Wallace in Stirling

The Scottish victory at Stirling Bridge came as a huge shock to the English, and doubtless to some in Scotland as well. With Surrey defeated and his army in tatters, men all across Scotland joined the rebel cause. Nobles who had previously sworn fealty to Edward turned coat and raised bands of soldiers to fight against him.

With momentum on his side, Wallace went on the offensive against England, and by the end of October 1297, he had invaded English territory by marching his growing army into Northumberland and taking its inhabitants by surprise. From Northumberland, Wallace led his men across the northwest of England, arriving as far as Cockermouth. While it sounds particularly bold, Wallace was at least partly forced to march into England because Scotland was stricken by famine and his army, which had grown markedly in size, needed more resources.

It was during this period that Wallace earned the reputation among the English as a ruthless and violent brute. Without siege machines, the Scottish army could not take any English cities of consequence, so they resorted to raiding and pillaging less-protected towns. According to Walter of Guisborough, "the services of God totally ceased in all the monasteries and churches between Newcastle and Carlisle, for all the canons, monks and priests fled before the face of the Scots, as did nearly all the people." The reputation for ferocity and barbarity that Wallace gained at this time remained with him for centuries after his death, even though, as Andrew Fisher claims, the cruel acts he ordered were "like those ordered by Edward I at Berwick," and were "of a kind often repeated by both sides." By late November, after a failed attempt to raid the bishopric of Durham, the severe weather forced the end of the invasion of England. Wallace and his troops returned north.

Using his title of Guardian of the Realm, Wallace tried to reestablish order in Scotland in the name of John I, but despite a growing mass of popular support, he was undermined by a lack of support from the nobility. Many Scottish nobles resented Wallace's quick rise to power, and according to some contemporaries, Wallace didn't hesitate to use harsh measures against his detractors at home. Stories of imprisonment and hangings made the rounds in both Scotland and England, confirming in the eyes of the English Wallace's status as a violent brigand. In fact, it was a shared sentiment that Wallace should be defeated that brought the English people together in support of their monarch's renewed campaign in Scotland. In the winter of 1297-1298, Edward had been in Flanders overseeing his campaign against France, and he did not return to England until March 1298 after a truce was negotiated with the French. Almost immediately, he set about preparing for war with the Scots and even transferred the seat of government north to York in order to be closer to his target. In April, he convened a war council in York to plan a campaign, but the Scottish magnates ordered to attend ignored his directive. In retaliation, Edward announced the forfeiture of their lands.

On June 25, the king's army assembled at Roxburgh, and Edward joined them by early July. Edward headed a strong force composed of roughly 2,000-3,000 horsemen and about 14,000 infantry, many of whom were Welsh, but as he led the army north and advanced into Scotland through Lauderdale, he found the land devastated and empty of inhabitants, which deprived him of the opportunity to gain intelligence about the Scottish army's whereabouts.

While Edward's preparations for war are well known, Wallace's own actions during this time are far less understood. In fact, it is impossible to place him between his return to Scotland in November 1297, following the raid of northern England, and March 1298, when documents show his presence at Porphichen in Linlithgowshire on March 29th. However, these documents also reveal that by March 1298, Wallace had two new titles: knight and guardian of the kingdom, both in addition to his already established role as leader of the army. He was the first Scot to be the sole holder of the second title, guardian of the kingdom. The dates he received these titles are unknown, but it's safe to assume the military prowess he exhibited throughout 1297 was the reason they were bestowed on him. Of course, to Edward, Wallace's titles meant nothing.

By the summer of 1298, Edward's sole aim was to locate and subsequently annihilate Sir William and his motley army, but Wallace was not eager to engage in battle with the English and thus engaged in a shrewd strategy of withdrawal, heading ever farther north and leaving nothing but scorched earth behind him. Edward took the bait and continued advancing deeper into Scotland, overstretching his lines of communication and supplies just as Wallace had hoped. Unable to locate the enemy or live off the land, his army was soon starving and in disarray. On July 19, when the army was at Temple Liston, a large supply of wine reached them, and Edward promptly distributed it. The Welsh soldiers became drunk and ended up rioting, killing several priests. Edward unleashed his cavalry on them, and 80 Welsh soldiers were killed. Many others threatened to change sides before the outbreak was finally quelled. Following this clash, Edward decided to retire to Edinburgh. Wallace's strategy was working, and he was yet again outwitting King Edward.

Edward was on the verge of retreat when fortune finally smiled on him on July 21; two earls had a messenger convey intelligence to the king that Wallace and his men were stationed at Falkirk, less than 20 miles away. The messenger also informed Edward of Wallace's intention to attack the retreating English army by night. Edward acted at once and immediately directed his army toward Falkirk. That night they camped near the Scottish forces, and the king ordered his men to sleep with their horses beside them in case the Scots attacked. Chaos soon ensued when Edward himself was injured by his horse and the soldiers panicked, and it was only by mounting his horse to display his strength that the king was able to calm his men. At sunrise the next morning, he led his army toward Falkirk.

Edward came upon Wallace in a strongly entrenched position, protected by a morass which was hidden from the English. Though Wallace had attempted to avoid battle, he at least found himself in a strong position when Edward surprised him with his men arranged to fight. When the English spotted them, the Scots were divided into four schiltroms, the core Scottish battle strategy. A schiltrom was a formation of as many as 2,000 men brandishing 12 foot-long spears and gathered in either huge circles or rectangles to look something like a lethal hedgehog. The ranks of the schiltrom were to be packed tightly so as to be nearly impenetrable. With this formation, the Scottish infantry could face off against mounted cavalrymen, England's strongest weapon. Between the schiltroms, Wallace had stationed his archers, and behind everyone stood the modest-sized Scottish cavalry, under the command of John Comyn.

Despite having a clear advantage, as well as the benefit of the element of surprise, Edward preferred not to engage immediately and instructed his army to rest. However, several men, including the earls of Norfolk, Hereford, and Lincoln, refused to follow his order and led a unit forward toward the Scots. They were blocked from advancing further by the morass and had to shift westward, splitting into two wings. Once past the marshland, the English vanguard clashed with the schiltroms, who held their positions and managed to inflict heavy damage on the English cavalry. In response, Edward called up his archers to weaken the Scottish ranks.

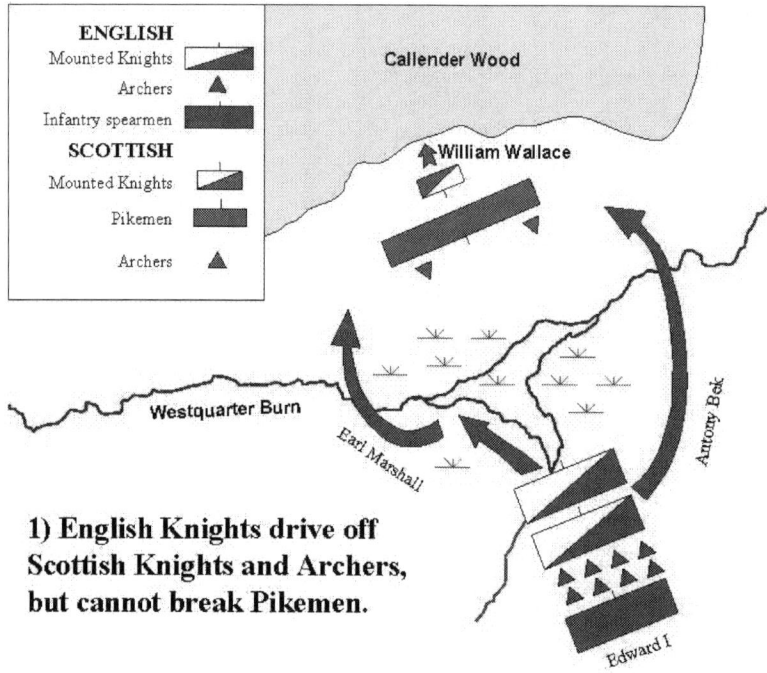

Map of the early action at Falkirk made by Mike Young

When Edward called up the archers, the Scottish cavalry fled, leaving the schiltroms and the Scottish archers with no rear support, but even with a barrage of arrows falling on them, the schiltroms managed to keep their discipline. While they were suffering heavy losses, they also killed more than 100 English horsemen, but Wallace was severely weakened without his cavalry, which became even more evident once Edward withdrew his cavalry and advanced his longbowmen and crossbowmen. The Scottish infantry was massacred by both the hail of arrows and a series of renewed cavalry assaults.

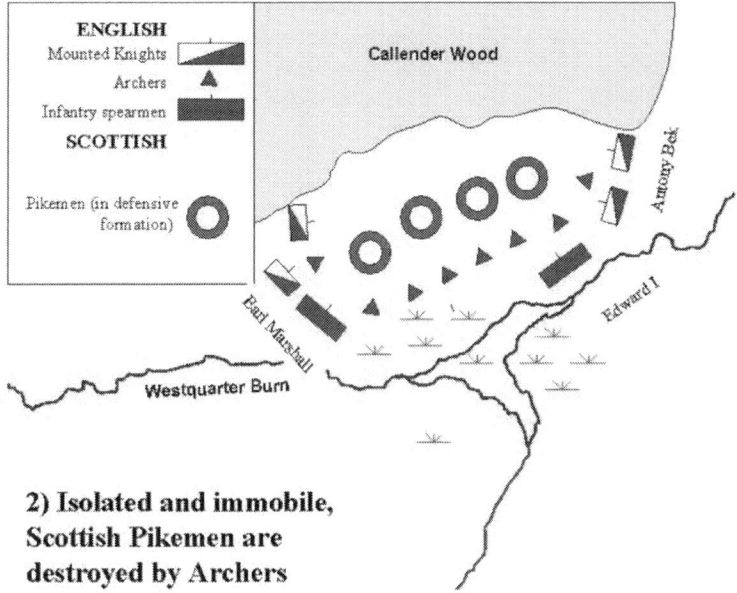

2) Isolated and immobile, Scottish Pikemen are destroyed by Archers

Map by Mike Young

Wallace left the field with a small force before the battle was over, but while the English charged him with cowardice, he was apparently working to ensure the escape of Scottish survivors, many of whom fled into the nearby woods. Wallace headed toward Stirling and burnt the town and the castle once he arrived. Though Edward had won at Falkirk, his army was too depleted to carry on the campaign or to pursue Wallace, so he began to withdraw his troops and was back in Carlisle by September 9.

With that, Edward's fight for Scotland was temporarily suspended, and the same could be said for Wallace. Sometime between the battle of Falkirk and the following December, Wallace resigned the guardianship, which was taken over by Robert the Bruce and John Comyn. He traveled to the European continent, where he presented Scotland's case for freedom to various courts.

As it turned out, diplomacy proved to be nearly as dangerous as warfare. It is difficult to know for certain where Wallace went first, and some believe he visited Norway before arriving in France in early November 1299 to lobby for King Philip IV's support. What is clear though is that rather than listening to Wallace's case, Philip had him arrested and offered to hand him over to the English. The cause of the king's sudden loyalty to the English, his former enemies, was Edward's marriage to his sister Margaret only two months earlier. However, when Edward learned that Wallace was in French captivity, he responded with a surprising lack of interest and urgency. He merely thanked Philip and requested that he keep Wallace in France until further notice.

There is no clear explanation for Edward's apparent apathy, and speculation suggests that the English king was not bent on Wallace's destruction. Perhaps he considered the Scot too removed and far from the Scottish cause and thus no longer a real threat, but whatever Edward's thinking, he made absolutely no attempt to have Wallace brought to England for justice. After a year of watching over Wallace, Philip grew fond of him and released him to carry on his diplomatic campaigns elsewhere.

Though Edward had broken the Scottish army, the result was not the total conquest he hoped for. Political opposition from a group of English magnates forced him to withdraw with the job half done. The English now controlled large swathes of Scotland, mostly centered around castles in the south and east, but just like the Scottish kings before them, they had a harder time controlling the highlands and islands. Scotland was conquered in theory, but the flames of rebellion burned on.

Wallace's army was broken, and with it any claim he had to political authority. In his place the Scots appointed a pair of guardians: Robert the Bruce and John Comyn, Lord of Badenoch, who had supported Balliol in the disputed succession. William Lamberton, the Bishop of St Andrews, was later added as a third guardian to mediate between the two men, who seldom saw eye to eye. Under this new leadership, the Scots returned to a strategy of raids and ambushes rather than trying to engage the English in pitched battle. There followed several years of small struggles and minor engagements in which the future of Scotland remained uncertain.

In England, the elderly Edward was facing a range of political challenges. Asking for money to fund his wars always created some resistance from the nobles and clergy, on whom the burden of payment mostly rested, and Edward's authoritarian leadership style was also leading to some resentment and calls for the reassertion of noble rights. Like many English monarchs, he had troubles with senior clergymen; the English church and its priests might owe some allegiance as Englishmen to the King, but they also owed allegiance to the Pope and had a duty to defend the church against royal encroachments. Churchmen sometimes resisted Edward's demands of taxes or appointed priests to new positions in line with papal rather than royal policy. When Archbishop Corbridge of York did this in 1304, it led to an angry confrontation, the King letting no man put a foreign Pope ahead of him. Arguments with the church subsided with political changes in Europe and the appointment of the pro-English Pope Clement V in 1305, but the conflict between how churchmen saw their loyalties and how their monarchs did would remain a constant throughout the Middle Ages.

The greatest source of conflict between Edward and the papacy became Scotland. Pressure from the French led him to release the deposed John Balliol into the Pope's custody in 1299, but this was not the end of church intervention. The Papal Bull Scimus, Fili condemned the English occupation of Scotland and demanded that the English withdraw, a demand that Edward completely ignored.

While Edward was occupied with affairs at home, the Scots blockaded Stirling Castle, forcing the English garrison to surrender after they ran out of food. In May 1300, Edward launched yet another campaign in Scotland to bring the country under his permanent control. He focused in particular on securing the castles, and after invading Galloway, he laid siege to Caerlaverock castle near the southern coast south of Dumfries. Siege engines were transported from Lochmaben and surrounding castles in order to force out the 60 Scots trying to defend the stronghold against the much larger English army, and once Edward finally broke through the defenses, he hanged several of the Scottish fighters from the castle's battlements. However, aside from a few other minor skirmishes, the English campaign of 1300 achieved little else of significance beside rebuke from outsiders; that August, the papacy sent a letter imploring Edward to withdraw from Scotland.

Over the spring and summer of the next four years, 1301-1304, Edward continued to lead campaigns north into Scotland with the view of bringing the territory definitively under his control, and in 1302, his authority increased when Robert the Bruce submitted to him. Later the same year, even the papacy softened its stance on his place in Scottish affairs, as Pope Boniface VIII wrote to the Scottish bishops encouraging them to reconcile with Edward. As his hold over Scotland grew more secure, Edward resurrected old practices, such as demanding that the Scottish nobles pay homage to him. He also reestablished an English administration, including English sheriffs in all strategic localities, to run several aspects of Scotland's political and legal systems.

Portrait of Pope Boniface VIII

During Edward's operations in 1303, however, he experienced difficulties early on due to sustained opposition posed by Wallace, who repeatedly hindered both divisions of the English army from advancing. The king and his men eventually made his way across most of Scotland before settling for the winter near Dunfermline, and by early 1304, the tides turned in Edward's favor. On February 9, John Comyn submitted to him, followed by all of the leading and influential Scots except Wallace and a few others. Perhaps one of the reasons Wallace didn't submit is because it wasn't a palatable option; had Wallace chosen to submit to Edward, he would not have enjoyed the same lenient terms granted to both Bruce and Comyn because Edward all but excluded him from this option: "as for Sir William Wallace, it is agreed that he may render himself up to the will and mercy of our sovereign lord the king, if it shall seem good to him." In other words, if Wallace surrendered, no clemency was guaranteed.

The invasion of 1303-4 was to be Edward I's last successful act of conquest. Now in his 60s, he was very old by the standards of the time, but still determined to lead his forces in the field. Marching in strength through Dundee, Brechin and Aberdeen, the English drove into the heartland of Scotland, proving the inability of the Scots to hold against a large English force. Having advanced as far north as Moray, they returned to Dunfermline for the winter. Comyn, as Guardian of Scotland, could not muster enough forces to match them.

In January 1304 the Scottish nobility, led by Comyn, surrendered to Edward. As part of the surrender, Edward agreed that the country's laws and the rights of the nobles would be as they had been under King Alexander. This was a very different surrender from the one that had come before. Edward was diplomatic rather than menacing, returning lands to the lords who surrendered to his rule and agreeing to the formation of a new committee of both English and Scottish members who would decide how Scotland would be governed. Perhaps having learned a lesson from responses to his previous harshness, or perhaps seeing that his son would need a different approach to keep the Scots in line, Edward used the carrot as well as the stick.

With nearly all of the powerful Scots in his back pocket and Stirling castle now in his possession, Edward intensified his efforts to capture the elusive Wallace. In March 1304, he had sent a large force, which included Robert the Bruce, to fight against the Scottish hero, but it failed to capture him.

Pope Boniface VIII, who had fallen out with Philip IV of France and now needed the English King's backing, supported Edward's occupation. He ordered the Scottish bishops, many of whom had been among the lords leading the revolt, to join in obedience to the conquering king.

The last bastion of Scottish resistance was at Stirling Castle, where the garrison refused to accept the new order. From April to July 1304, Edward laid siege to the castle. In one of the most spectacular pieces of showboating in medieval warfare, gunpowder, a rarity at the time, was used to make Greek fire. Massive siege machines were ordered, including the colossal trebuchet Warwolf, a masterpiece of the siege engineer's art that earned its creator Thomas Greenfield the substantial sum of £40. A viewing gallery was constructed so that ladies of the English court could watch the siege as it played out. The English combined bombardment with cutting off Scottish supply lines, leaving the castle's garrison starving and shaken.

Always looking to lead from the front, Edward took part in the siege, and his life was twice put in jeopardy, once when a crossbow bolt pierced his clothes and once when a stone from a mangonel scared his horse into throwing him. Grey haired but still determined, the aging king responded to the locals' resistance by having the lead stripped from church roofs for the counterweights of his siege machines.

Short of supplies and without hope of relief, the Stirling garrison eventually asked to surrender. Edward did not allow them to do so until Warwolf had been completed and tested against their walls. That done, and despite earlier threats, he let the 30 men of the garrison leave with their lives. Only their leader, Sir William Oliphant, was sent to the Tower of London, and only an Englishman who had given the castle to the Scots was executed.

During a skirmish in September 1304, Wallace again managed to escape the English army, but only after inflicting considerable casualties on the army. In response, Edward increased the stakes with bribery and coercion by promising several Scots who had submitted to him, including Comyn, to commute their sentences of exile in return for Wallace's capture.

Despite the intense pressure on Wallace, it would take Edward nearly another full year to find and detain him. How he lived at large until then is unknown, as no documents make reference to his movements or actions, but on August 3, 1305, Edward finally got his wish when Wallace was taken by one of his fellow Scots, John Menteith, the keeper of Dumbarton Castle. Menteith was rewarded with land for his compliance.

Edward refused to meet with Wallace following his arrest and had him transported to London on August 22. In the early morning of the next day, Wallace arrived and was taken on horseback in a procession of judicial and legal authorities to Westminster Hall. There was frenzied excitement on the streets as many Londoners came out to catch a glimpse of the notorious Scottish warrior.

Inside the hall, Wallace was accompanied onto a scaffold, where officials placed a laurel crown on his head in an apparent attempt to humiliate him by deeming him merely a king of outlaws, as it was the only crown they believed he merited. The justice presiding over the "trial" presented the indictment, accusing Wallace of treason and engaging in war crimes by "sparing neither age nor sex, monk nor nun." While admitting to the other allegations, Wallace denied the charge of treason, replying, "I could not be a traitor to Edward, for I was never his subject." No examination of evidence took place, nor was any testimony of witness heard; Wallace was not permitted to defend himself because his legal status was that of an outlawed thief.

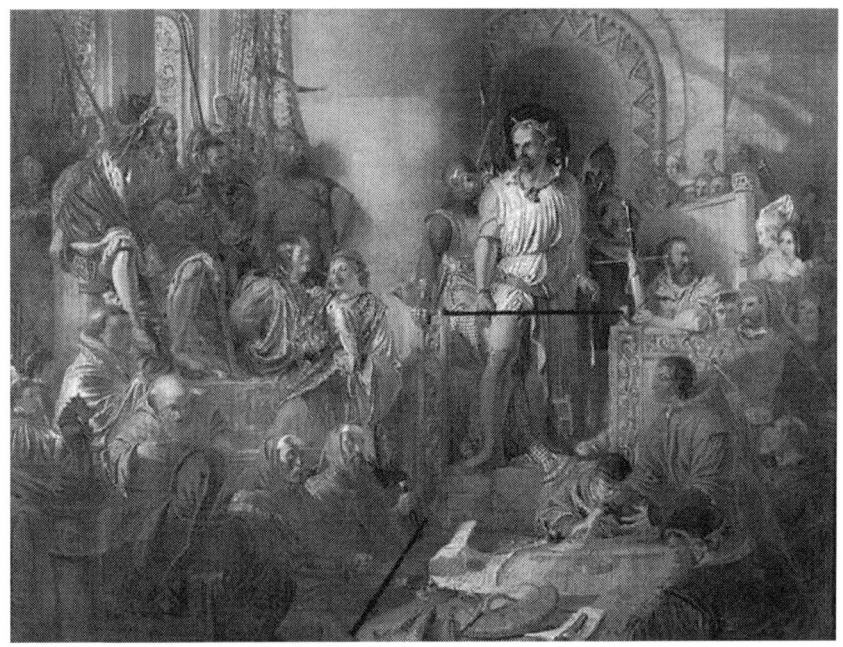

Daniel Maclise's painting, *The Trial of William Wallace at Westminster*

Obviously, the proceedings were a mere formality, and the judgment was given on the same day. William Wallace was found guilty of treason against the English king for taking up arms against him in Scotland and for making an alliance with France, and he received the standard sentence for treason. He was to be drawn to the gallows on a hurdle by horses through the streets of London, where he would be hanged for the crimes of murder and robbery. As a desecrator of churches, he was to be cut down from the gallows while not quite dead in order that his internal organs and genitals be removed and burned. Finally, as an outlaw, his head was cut off and placed on London Bridge, while the remainder of his body was to be cut into quarters to be displayed in Newcastle, Berwick, Stirling, and Perth. As historian John Reuben Davies put it, "Wallace's execution is a classic scene from one of history's great tragedies: the death of a national hero, a bloodthirsty judicial killing, the demonstrative and exemplary justice of an English king." A plaque now documents the spot near where he was executed on August 23, 1305.

In the decades following his death, Wallace's legacy fell under the shadow of the rising Bruce dynasty, and Wallace, who throughout his life had raised the banner in the name of the Scottish king John Balliol, was not a celebrated figure in Scotland during the Bruce years. It was Blind

Harry, 170 years later, who rescued Wallace from potential obscurity with his heavily embellished epic poem celebrating the great warrior's achievements. Had it not been for Blind Harry's account, Wallace might not have been remembered so prominently as a leading protagonist in the Scottish Wars of Independence. Paradoxically, however, while Harry salvaged the memory of Wallace, he also obscured it with his dressed up version of the Scot's life. It has become the task of historians of the 20th and 21st centuries to put Wallace back into perspective and to attempt to determine the real details of his life as best as possible with the scant evidence available.

If anything, the efforts to piece together Wallace's biography reveal how unnecessary it was to exaggerate his life's narrative. Even based on the little that is known, it's evident that Wallace was a unique figure in history. In a socially rigid society, he rose from modest beginnings to become the leader of Scotland, and though he lacked formal or extensive training in warfare, he fought more successfully than perhaps anyone else against one of the best military kings in history. His life story was already the stuff of legend, with no need for extra burnishing.

Chapter 7: The Rise of the Bruce

A Victorian depiction of leaders of the Scottish Wars of Independence

With Wallace out of the way, all of Scotland had been conquered, an achievement made possible as much by Edward's logistical prowess as by his warlike determination to win, but now a new settlement was needed to govern the country. At first glance, what followed continued Edward's more diplomatic approach to Scotland. The country would have its own Parliament, although laws made in England would be enforced. This would be done by the king's lieutenant, initially the King's nephew John of Brittany, and while this put an Englishman at the top of Scotland's government, many Scots were given senior positions. A council of Scottish nobles was set up to advise the lieutenant, and it included both John Comyn and Robert the Bruce. Involving them was a way of keeping potential resistance leaders in the English camp.

For all its conciliatory elements, the wording of the new settlement gave Scots reasons to be nervous and resentful. Scotland was referred to as a land, not a realm or kingdom, tearing away its status and independence. Laws were to be revised that the English King considered contrary to reason and the will of God, a definition whose broad scope, combined with Edward's personality, could open the door to the removal of many traditional Scottish rights. In more practical terms, key castles were to be held by English commanders, depriving the Scots of controls of these buildings of great strategic and symbolic status. They were to be allowed some measure of self-government, but behind it lay military occupation and the threat of further changes to come.

The Scottish nobility had given in, and the lowly knight Wallace was no more. At last, the English victory seemed complete, and Edward I, the Hammer of the Scots, could look with pride upon the island he had united by war. It was quite an inheritance to pass into the hands of his son.

A medieval depiction of Robert the Bruce

By this point, the Bruces, and Robert the Bruce in particular, had switched sides several times during Edward I's Scottish wars. Bruce had been involved in the half-hearted noble resistance that folded at Irvine, had been a Guardian of Scotland during a period of resistance, and had switched back to Edward's side during the final act of conquest. His lack of loyalty to either the Scottish resistance or the English occupation could be seen as fickle, but in reality it reflected his constancy in furthering a single cause, the same cause that motivated most of the medieval nobility: the fortunes of his family.

Whether out of family loyalty, self-interest as heir to that family's power, or some mingling of the two, Bruce's actions make sense as steps taken in protecting his family's lands, wealth, status and claim to the throne. These interests often came into conflict, and when the throne was a distant dream he would side with the English in order to prevent Edward seizing his lands. When the Scots grew strong and there was a chance to show what kind of leader he was, what kind of Scottish king he could make, or even a chance to take on a role as a leader of the nobility and Guardian of the realm, he rallied to that cause. At the same time, when Scottish independence began to look more like a reality, and when the interests of other would-be kings such as the Balliols looked increasingly secure, he fell out with his domestic opponents, causing frictions in government and returning to Edward's side.

The settlement that followed the 1304 surrender undid many of Bruce's hopes. The Kingdom of Scotland was no more. Even at his most agreeable, Edward I had settled on ending the nation's independence rather than installing a client king, a position Bruce might have hoped to be given after siding with the English. Despite their support of the English King, the family's lands were not all restored.

Bruce, disillusioned at not having been rewarded as he had hoped, may have begun considering rebellion as early as June 1304, when he and William Lamberton made a pact to support each other against all men. By the following year, Edward apparently did not trust him, ordering Bruce to put Kildrummy Castle into someone else's hands in September. In October he took back lands he had given to Bruce only six months before, lands taken from Sir Gilbert de Umfraville. If the King hoped that such punishments would ensure Bruce's obedience, then he had sorely misjudged the man; these events only hardened Bruce's resolve, giving him less interest in continuing English rule and more reason to rebel.

The settlement that caused him so much frustration also created an opportunity for this ambitious noble. By removing Balliol as King once and for all, Edward created a vacuum in the Scottish leadership, a space into which Bruce could step. If there was no Scottish monarch, then he was free to assume that role. Growing resentment against the English treatment of Scotland further ensured that when the time came, there would plenty of people willing to flock to Bruce's banner.

Within the Scottish nobility, Bruce's main competitor for the throne was John Comyn. While Bruce had gone back and forth in his allegiances, Comyn had been more solid in his resistance to English rule. The most powerful noble in Scotland, and a man connected to many great families on both sides of the border, Comyn was in many ways a more credible candidate for rebel leader than Bruce.

These two great Scottish nobles had argued in the past, but events came to a head in February 1306. That month they met in the chapel of Greyfriars Monastery in Dumfries to discuss their political future. It is possible that they had a previous agreement to put Bruce on the throne, which Comyn then betrayed, or Comyn may simply have refused Bruce the support he wanted. Regardless of the details of their disagreement, Bruce murdered Comyn in the church, stabbing him to death in front of the altar.

A 19th century depiction of the murder

The die was now cast. Bruce could risk everything to become King of Scotland, or he could face the justice meted out by Edward I, a man he had no reason to trust and who had shown great savagery in dealing with troublesome Scots. Thus, the next great Scottish uprising began not with a clash between English and Scots but with one Scotsman spilling another's blood on holy ground.

After killing Comyn and facing off against his supporters in the Greyfriars graveyard, Bruce led his men in an attack on Dumfries Castle, after which the garrison swiftly surrendered. From there he rode on to Glasgow, where he confessed to the sacrilegious murder before Bishop Robert Wishart. Wishart granted Bruce absolution and called upon the Scottish clergy to support him in his bid to take the throne and throw out the English. Though he had the support of clergymen in Scotland, Bruce was soon excommunicated by the Pope at the request of Edward I; the church in Scotland had his back, but not the church as a whole.

At Scone on March 25, Bruce was crowned King of the Scots by William Lamberton, the Bishop of St Andrews. He was then crowned again by Isabella Macduff, Countess of Buchan, whose family had traditionally had the right to crown Scottish kings.

Following the murder of Comyn, Bruce found himself fighting a civil war in Scotland, with his own supporters battling with those of the Comyns. It was into this mix that Edward sent the initial English response, led by Aymer de Valence, Comyn's brother-in-law. In April 1306, Edward appointed Valence to raise an army to fight the Scots, and in May the English King knighted his son and 250 other men in a solemn ceremony to mark the launch of the war. He vowed to avenge Comyn's death, and the new knights followed him in taking this dramatic public oath.

Valence acted quickly and headed to Perth, where he rallied many of Comyn's supporters around him. Bruce arrived at Perth in June, and the traditional roles of English and Scottish combatants were reversed. It was Bruce who called upon Valence to meet him in open battle, and Valence who first refused and then led a surprise dawn raid against the Scots at the encampment at Methven, soundly beating them. Following the disaster at Methven, Bruce took a leaf from Wallace's book and fled to the hills, hiding out over the winter with a small band of his most loyal followers.

Despite his failing physical health, Edward I was determined to join in the war, and in the autumn he began the journey north. However, before he could reach Scotland he collapsed at Lanercost Priory in Cumberland. Unable to continue his journey, he spent the winter at the Priory, where glass was installed in the windows to keep him warm. Undeterred, Edward I was not a man to let the failings of his own body stand in his way. In March 1307, despite having trouble even walking, he held a Parliament at Carlisle, once more asserting his dominance over his subjects.

While Edward was mustering the strength to rise from his sick bed, Bruce was fashioning a new plan to defeat the English and their supporters among the Comyn faction. Emerging from hiding in February 1307, he set up operations in the Earldom of Carrick, lands belonging to his family and where he knew he was likely to receive support. Having learned at Methven that he could not beat the English in an open battle, he used the guerilla tactics previously utilized by Wallace and Murray. Launching fast, small hit-and-run raids against the English, he made it harder for them to hold the territory they claimed to rule as food supplies were taken or destroyed rather than left where the English could use them to feed their armies. He avoided facing those armies, withdrawing in the face of their approach, knowing that they would most likely return south when winter came and that his best hope was to wait them out.

Bruce's first success came in a small battle in April, when he ambushed an English force trying to attack his camp at Glen Trool, a victory that boosted his side's morale. He then slipped through the English forces encircling him and gathered more troops before taking up position at Loudon Hill in Ayrshire. It was a location carefully chosen for the Scottish King's first field battle of his renewed campaign. The location was a good defensive one, and the ground was prepared in advance of battle by the Scots. When Valence led a force to attack them there on

May 10, the English found themselves funneled by marshes and ditches into a narrow space at the bottom of the hill. This left them disorganized and crammed in together, unable to resist when the Scottish spearmen advanced down the hill upon them. The English were defeated and Valence fled. King Robert had his first battlefield victory.

The English responded to this defeat with a renewed cruelty, as prisoners taken in the campaign were sent south to be hung, drawn and quartered, but the invaders had again misjudged the character of the people they were up against. Far from making the Scots give in out of fear, these actions raised resentment against the English and broadened Bruce's base of support.

On July 3, Edward I set off to put down this latest insurrection by men he saw as rebellious subjects. Despite suffering from dysentery on top of his ongoing health problems, the King insisted on riding a horse at the head of his army rather than being carried in a litter, even though he could only travel this way for two miles a day. The bold gesture slowed down the English army and did nothing to help the King's health. On July 7, at a hamlet near the border between England and Scotland on the Solway Firth, Edward I passed away. Nearly 70 years old, he died as he had lived, seeking to crush his opponents.

It was said that as he lay dying, Edward gave one last request to his son that after his death, the flesh should be boiled from his bones for burial and the bones then carried into battle against the Scots. He did not want even death to keep him from completing the task upon which he spent so many years and spilled so much blood.

However, it was not to be; though it was not obvious at the time, the death of the Hammer of the Scots also saw the death of England's chances of holding Scotland. As English kings go, Edward II was about as different as it could get. He was vacillating rather than authoritative, disinterested in war, and vulnerable to the influence of those close to him. The reign of Edward II weakened England and saw it torn apart by civil conflict, but even before these problems came to fruition, the change of monarchs created opportunities for Bruce.

A contemporary depiction of Edward II being crowned

Edward II was not interested in continuing his father's campaign in Scotland, or in launching another one any time soon. Between 1307 and 1310, the English never went on the offensive, leaving the initiative in Scottish hands. Without English intervention, Bruce was able to focus on winning his civil war with the Comyns. Capturing a string of castles from Comyn adherents, he built up a power base before marching deep into the territory of John Comyn, Earl of Buchan, the leader of that faction. During this campaign, Bruce fell ill, and he was known by many to be unwell. An attack by Buchan's forces triggered the Battle of Inverurie on May 23 1308, but Bruce's surprise appearance on the battlefield played a part in shaking the morale of Buchan's forces, leading to a decisive victory for Bruce.

Following the battle, Robert the Bruce ordered one of the most brutal actions of the wars, known as the Harrying of Buchan. Much of the population of that region was loyal to the Comyns, providing them with a solid base of support. To remove this support, and with it his leading opponent, Bruce had the region pillaged. Castles were destroyed and their inhabitants massacred, making it impossible for the Comyns to defend those lands. Similar actions in Argyle and Kintyre weakened another opposing clan, the Macdougalls, who he then defeated at the Battle of Pas of Brander.

By March 1309 Bruce, now King Robert I, had gone from being a wanted fugitive to the leading power in Scotland. He held his first Parliament, an act that asserted his authority, made clear who was on his side, and showed that Scotland truly had its own King once more. By August, he controlled all the land north of the River Tay, and the following year a general council of the Scottish clergy formally recognized him as King, an important moment in an era when secular and spiritual authority were deeply intertwined.

With Scotland under control, Bruce turned his attention to driving out the English. Over the next five years, castle after castle was besieged and taken back. Linlithgow, Dumbarton, Dumfries and Roxburgh all fell. Perth was stormed in an assault led by King Robert himself, wading through the freezing waters of the moat. Edinburgh, one of Scotland's most important cities, was taken in 1314.

As well as wearing down the English garrisons still stationed in Scotland, King Robert began attacking England itself. Starting in 1311, Scottish raids pillaged the north of England, carrying away wealth, food and supplies to support their war. While psychologically it was doubtless cathartic for the Scots to pillage the country that had done them so much harm, the strategic value came in supporting the war effort north of the border and in undermining the authority of the English King. If Edward II could not defend his own people, there was less reason for anyone in Scotland to side with him or for Englishmen to fight for him against the Scots.

All the while, these successes still came from a strategy of avoiding pitch battles in which the English would have the upper hand, but the damage the Scots were doing led to mounting pressure on Edward II to act. The event that finally stirred him to action and triggered one of the most famous battles in Scottish history was yet another siege of the strategically crucial Stirling Castle. Control of Stirling meant control not only of a substantial fortified base, but of that vital crossing of the Forth that had been the scene of Wallace's greatest victory.

A statute of Robert the Bruce at Stirling Castle

Starting in 1313, King Robert's brother Edward laid siege to the castle, which was still in English hands. Cut off from supplies, the constable of the castle negotiated an agreement with Edward Bruce that if no relief force arrived by midsummer 1314, the garrison would surrender. This took pressure off the younger Bruce to expend his men's lives in an assault and created a dim light at the end of the tunnel for the beleaguered English garrison. It also lit a fire beneath Edward II, who mustered an army and marched north.

To King Robert, few prizes were worth the risk of an open battle against the numerically stronger and better equipped English, but Stirling Castle was one of them. For Edward II, it was not just of value in holding onto Scotland; he was facing political opposition at home from a group of lords led by the Earl of Lancaster, and a victory against the Scots would help him in his struggle against them. Though Lancaster and some of these other lords refused the call to join his army, Edward marched north with all speed, hoping to relieve Stirling before it was too late.

It was an exhausting march, during which the army took only short breaks for rest and food, and the difficulty was made worse by damage done to the Scottish roads to slow them down. Tired and demoralized, the English arrived in sight of Stirling on the evening of June 23, where they found themselves facing a Scottish army half their size. Two English scouting parties were driven back before the armies settled down for the night, with the English forced to camp in marshy ground.

As the sun rose the following day, the two sides prepared to continue this fateful engagement. The Battle of Bannockburn, named for a stream on the battlefield, was unevenly matched. The English outnumbered the Scots 2-1, and more than that in terms of the armored men-at-arms who formed the hard hitting core of the era's armies. On a leadership level, the mismatch went the other way; Edward II was not a strong leader, and a dispute between the Earls of Gloucester and Hereford over who should lead the vanguard undermined the army's sense of purpose and its tactics. At one point in the battle, Gloucester led a suicidal charge against the Scottish ranks, a courageous but desperate act that led to his death rather than the assertion of authority he had desired.

An illustration depicting Robert the Bruce addressing troops before the battle

What mattered most was that Bruce was well prepared, having once again carefully chosen the ground on which to fight. The English could not bring their numbers to bear in overwhelming the Scots. Marshy ground made it difficult for the English to advance and weakened the effectiveness of cavalry charges. The use of defensive spear schiltrons allowed the Scots to advance while also defending against English attacks, and those attacks went from useless to disastrous. After a horse was killed from under him, Edward II fled the field, and lacking what little leadership they had, his army broke.

Bannockburn was a complete disaster for the English. Over a thousand men were lost, including 22 nobles and 68 knights, and the King's privy seal, used to authenticate documents, fell into Scottish hands. The Scots suffered around 500 casualties but were victorious against the odds, and Stirling Castle was theirs.

A 14ᵗʰ century English depiction of the battle

Though it was far from the last battle in the wars for Scottish independence, Bannockburn was the decisive one. Never again would the English come so close to conquering their northern neighbors. Seven years after his death, Edward I's work had been completely undone.

Chapter 8: Robert the Bruce's Reign

A depiction of Robert the Bruce being crowned King of Scots

With the English in retreat, Bruce now led the Scots in going on the offensive. They launched raids into northern England, pillaging Yorkshire and Lancashire and driving back English forces sent against them. Local communities were given a choice - buy off the Scots or face the merciless pillaging of their property. It was a strategy that required great discipline in the Scottish army, both to march quickly through England and to ensure that the peace was kept when it was bought. Its purpose was both to fund the war and to undermine English authority, in the hopes that Edward would have to accept Scottish independence, something he refused to do during failed peace talks of October to November 1314. But England's major power centers of wealth, power and aristocratic culture lay in the south-east, and this devastation of the north was not enough to win major concessions from an English king.

Though Robert's position as King was secure, his dynasty was not. He and his wife had had no success in having a child, and his only descendant was Marjorie, the daughter of his first marriage. His royal line was further endangered on 2 March 1316 when Marjorie, then in the last month of a pregnancy, was thrown by her horse and killed. But the child amazingly survived, born by a hasty Caesarian section, and this grandson would go on to become King Robert II.

In 1315, Bruce sent forces across the sea to Ireland, then suffering from English attempts at domination. Supposedly an effort to free the Irish from the English, this allowed the Scots to open another front in their own fight against England. As a result of his efforts there, Robert's brother Edward Bruce was made High King of Ireland in 1316, and a later Scottish campaign in Ireland under Robert was as much about maintaining his brother's position as causing problems for the English.

Much like his position as King of the Scots, Bruce's attempt to gain dominance over Ireland was supported by rhetoric grounded in history and nationalist ideology. He viewed Ireland and Scotland as in some ways a single entity, with their shared Gaelic lineage and language, as distinct from the Anglo-Saxon population and Norman aristocracy of the English. The Kings of Leinster featured in Bruce's lineage through his ancestor Eva of Leinster, and his marriage alliance with the de Burgh family gave him connections to the northern Irish Earls of Ulster. By emphasizing these connections, he tried to build up the idea of a Scottish-Irish alliance in opposition to English domination of the British Isles. In a letter to Irish nobles he even referred to the two nations together as "nostra nacio" - "our nation" - and talked about recovering their ancient liberty.

This military and diplomatic campaign initially saw some success, especially in the north. But outside of Ulster, where marital connections to the Bruces gave nobles such as Donal O'Neil an interest in Scottish success, they never gained enough support to develop a strong hold. To those living in the south of Ireland, the Scots were indistinguishable from the English, just one more group of foreign soldiers come across the sea to invade their country. They brought with them the common woes of medieval warfare, the pain of destructive pillaging made worse by disruption to harvests and so growing famine. When Edward Bruce was killed at the Battle of Faughart on 14 October 1318, ending the Scottish efforts, Irish chroniclers were glad to see the end of this supposed attempt to free them from the English yoke.

Berwick remained in English hands for several years after Bannockburn, one last foreign bastion on Scottish soil. Repeated sieges and assaults failed to take it until 1318, when the Scots stormed the town and forced the garrison to retreat to the castle. These last English soldiers continued to resist for eleven weeks, but eventually surrendered on 18 June. Scotland was entirely in Scottish hands.

King Robert's campaign to thwart the English extended to other fronts, and diplomatically far beyond the British Isles. On 6 April 1320, 51 senior Scottish nobles set their seals to the Declaration of Arbroath, a letter to the Pope making the case for Bruce to be recognized and accepted as King of Scotland. This was a point of contention due to the continuing survival of John Balliol, the previous king. To justify Bruce's position, the Declaration put forward the argument that it was up to the people of Scotland, not just its King, to protect its liberty in the face of threats such as the English invasion, and that this extended to replacing the king if he proved unfit to defend his country. It was rhetoric and propaganda, not political philosophy, but it helped to win the Pope around to the side of the Scots. Some have argued that it was an early example of the principle of popular sovereignty - that a bad monarch should be overthrown by the people. But much like treating Magna Carta as a bastion of English liberties, this is about later readings, not the intent of the time. The people of Scotland whose rights the Declaration referred to were intended to be the powerful nobles who ran the country, and on whose support kings had always been reliant, not the masses of the nation at large.

Despite their earlier difficulties, Robert and his wife Elizabeth eventually had four children, including Robert's all-important son and heir David, born on March 5, 1324.

The English had never entirely conquered Scotland, and since Bannockburn they had been unable to claim any degree of control. But it was not until 1328 that they finally acknowledged Scotland's independence. The overthrow of Edward II the previous year had put his teenage son Edward III on the English throne, while the country was effectively ruled by the boy's mother Isabelle and her lover Roger Mortimer. Though Edward II had not been a popular king, the new regime also faced opposition and challenges over its legitimacy, Edward II having been dethroned and then vanished into prison, never to be seen again. Peace with Scotland was therefore a price worth paying, removing a threat from the northern border while Isabelle and Mortimer consolidated their power within England. In May 1328 Edward III signed the Treaty of Edinburgh-Northampton, and for the first time since his grandfather's reign, an English monarch officially recognized Scotland as an independent kingdom.

By the time the English recognized him as King, Robert Bruce was already suffering from the disease that would eventually kill him. It is impossible to tell with any certainty what this was, as even the classification of diseases in the period was different from our modern understanding. The claim by some chronicles that he was suffering from leprosy reflects the fact that any serious skin complaint was often given this label. If he had this disease then it is not reflected in the Scottish accounts of his death, and other possibilities include tuberculosis, syphilis, a series of strokes, or motor neuron disease. It seems that those around him did not believe it to be contagious, as there was no attempt to keep the King separate from others who might catch a disease off him.

Robert may have had this illness since as far back as 1306-9, when living on the run meant he suffered from cold and exposure during winters living outdoors. Whenever it began, by 1327 it had become serious, and was commented upon by someone who saw the King in Ulster in July that year, when he was so weak that he could barely move.

If Robert's physical health was in decline then his spiritual health was improving, at least by the standards of the age. In October 1328 the Pope lifted his excommunication and the interdict that had been laid on Scotland during the war with England. While such shifts in Papal viewpoint were politically motivated, the Pope wanting Scottish support for a crusade, they would have reassured many Scots that their immortal souls were no longer in jeopardy.

Around the same time, the ailing King began a final journey to find peace before his faltering body gave in. From his manor at Cardross he set out by ship to the Isle and Arran, where he spent the Christmas of 1328. He then sailed back to the mainland where he visited Turnberry Castle, once his own home as Earl of Carrick, and now occupied by his son and daughter-in-law, both of them still children. Carried overland form there on a litter, he arrived at Glenluce Abbey late in March 1329, and then went on to visit the shrine of Saint Ninian at Whithorn. There he fasted and prayed for several days. At the time, belief in the miraculous powers of saints was strong, and he may have hoped that Ninian could cure him of the illness which was clearly killing him. Alternatively, he may simply have wanted to make his peace with God after a life stained with blood and the dark turns of political scheming.

Having made his peace with the church and his family, King Robert sailed back to Cardross, where he dealt for one last time with the group who, more than any others, had been the beneficiaries and agents of his reign - the political nation of Scotland, in the form of its barons and prelates. These august persons were summoned to his bedside for one final council meeting. During the meeting, the King made great gifts to the religious houses and expressed his regret that he had never fulfilled his vow to go on crusade against the Muslims in the Holy Land. Perhaps hoping to ensure the safety of his soul by fulfilling this vow, or perhaps more concerned with consolidating his heroic reputation, he asked that his heart be cut out after his death and carried on crusade before returning to his homeland of Scotland.

Robert Bruce died on June 7, 1329, safe in the knowledge that he had achieved his goal of claiming the Kingdom of Scotland for the Bruces. He left his son David as King and his trusted lieutenant Moray as the boy's guardian. He was buried in spectacular style in the center of Dunfermline Abbey in a carved tomb decorated with gold leaf. In keeping with his final wish, his heart was removed before burial and placed in a silver casket to be borne on crusade. A planned international mission to the Holy Land failed to happen, so Sir James Douglas, wearing the casket on a chain around his neck, set out with a group of Scottish knights to join Alfonso XI of Castile's campaign against the kingdom of Granada in Moorish Spain. In August 1330, these Scottish knights fought in the Battle of Teba, helping Alfonso rout the Moorish forces there. Douglas threw Bruce's heart ahead of him into the enemy, and then followed his late king into battle one last time.

Dunfermline Abbey

Despite their heroism, the battle went badly for the Scots, and many of them, including Douglas, were killed. Though the battle was a Castilian victory, it did not prove decisive in the ongoing war for Spain. Thus, the surviving knights returned to Scotland, carrying with them King Robert's heart and Sir James Douglas' bones. At last Bruce's heart was laid to rest in Melrose Abbey in Roxburghshire, assuring that King Robert's heart dwells in death where it did in life: his beloved Scotland.

Online Resources

Other books about medieval England by Charles River Editors

Other books about the Middle Ages by Charles River Editors

Bibliography

Barrow, G. W. S. (1989), Kingship and Unity: Scotland 1000–1306, The New History of Scotland 2 (2nd ed.), Edinburgh: Edinburgh University Press, ISBN 0-7486-0104-X, 4th edition (2005) ISBN 0748620222

Barrow, G. W. S. (1976), Robert Bruce and the Community of the Realm of Scotland (2nd ed.), Edinburgh: Edinburgh University Press, ISBN 0-85224-307-3

Brown, Chris (2005), William Wallace. The True Story of Braveheart, Stroud: Tempus Publishing Ltd, ISBN 0-7524-3432-2

Brown, Michael (2004), The Wars of Scotland 1214–1371, The New Edinburgh History of Scotland 4, Edinburgh: Edinburgh University Press, ISBN 0-7486-1238-6

Balfour Paul, James (1904), The Scots Peerage, Edinburgh: David Douglas.

Bartlett, Robert (1993), The Making of Europe, Conquest, Colonization and Cultural Change: 950–1350, Princeton: Princeton University Press, ISBN 0-691-03298-X.

Bingham, Caroline (1998), Robert the Bruce, London: Constable, ISBN 0-09-476440-9.

Brown, Chris (2004), Robert the Bruce. A Life Chronicled, Stroud: Tempus, ISBN 0-7524-2575-7.

Brown, Chris (2008), Bannockburn 1314, Stroud: History, ISBN 978-0-7524-4600-4.

Cowan, Edward J., ed. (2007), The Wallace Book, Edinburgh: John Donald, ISBN 978-0-85976-652-4

Cowan, Edward J. (2007), "William Wallace: 'The Choice of the Estates'", in Cowan, Edward J., The Wallace Book, Edinburgh: John Donald, pp. 9–25, ISBN 978-0-85976-652-4

Dunbar, Archibald H. (1899), Scottish Kings 1005–1625, Edinburgh: D. Douglas, pp. 126–141, with copious original source materiéls.

Duncan, A. A. M. (2007), "William, Son of Alan Wallace: The Documents", in Cowan, Edward J., The Wallace Book, Edinburgh: John Donald, pp. 42–63, ISBN 978-0-85976-652-4

Duncan, A.A.M. (Editor), (1999) John Barbour: The Bruce Canongate.

Fawcett, Richard (ed.) (2005), Royal Dunfermline, Edinburgh: Society of Antiquaries of

Scotland, ISBN 978-0-903903-34-9.

Fisher, Andrew (2002), William Wallace (2nd ed.), Edinburgh: Birlinn, ISBN 1-84158-593-9

Grant, Alexander, (1984) Independence and Nationhood: Scotland 1306-1469 Edward Arnold. ISBN 978-0748602735.

Grant A, and Stringer, Keith J., (1995) Uniting the Kingdom? The Making of British History Routledge, pp. 97–108. ISBN 978-0415130417.

Hunter, Paul V (2012), The Adventures of Wee Robert Bruce, Bonhill, West Dunbartonshire: Auch Books.

Jardine, Henry (1821), Report relative to the tomb of King Robert the Bruce, and the cathedral church of Dunfermline, Edinburgh: Edinburgh Hay, Gall and Co..

Loudoun, Darren (2007), Scotlands Brave.

Mackenzie, Agnes Mure (1934), Robert Bruce, King of Scots

Macnamee, Colm (2006), The Wars of the Bruces: England and Ireland 1306–1328, Edinburgh: Donald, ISBN 978-0-85976-653-1.

Macnamee, Colm (2006), Robert Bruce: Our Most Valiant Prince, King and Lord, Edinburgh: Birlinn, ISBN 978-1-84158-475-1.

Morton, Graeme. William Wallace. London: Sutton, 2004. ISBN 0-7509-3523-5.

Nicholson, R., Scotland in the Later Middle Ages.

Oxford Dictionary of National Biography.

Ó Néill, Domhnall (1317), "Remonstrance of the Irish Chiefs to Pope John XXII", CELT archive.

Penman, Michael. Robert the Bruce: King of the Scots (2014)

Penman, Michael (2009), 'Robert Bruce's Bones: Reputations, Politics and Identities in Nineteenth-Century Scotland', International Review of Scottish Studies, 34 (2009), 7-73, Ontario: Centre for Scottish Studies at the University of Guelph.

Prestwich, Michael (1997). Edward I. New Haven: Yale University Press. ISBN 0-300-07209-0..

Reese, Peter. William Wallace: A Biography. Edinburgh: Canongate, 1998. ISBN 0-86241-

607-8.

Stead, Michael J., and Alan Young. In the Footsteps of William Wallace. London: Sutton, 2002.

Traquair, Peter (1998), Freedom's Sword, University of Virginia: Roberts Rinehart Publishers, ISBN 1570982473

Watson, Fiona, J. (1998), Under the Hammer: Edward I and Scotland, 1286-1307, Tuckwell Press, East Linton.

Printed in Great Britain
by Amazon